Now You Know Science

What's It Made Of?

Terry Jennings

W

FRANKLIN WATTS
LONDON•SYDNEY

This edition 2013

First published in 2009 by Franklin Watts

Franklin Watts
338 Euston Road, London NW1 3BH

Franklin Watts Australia
Level 17/207 Kent St, Sydney, NSW 2000

Created by Tagline   Ionor Head

ISBN: 978 1 4451 2322 6

Dewey classification: 620.1'1

A CIP catalogue for this book is available from the British Library.

Picture credits
t=top b=bottom l=left m=middle r=right

3, 23, 28tr, Shutterstock, Inc; 5, Shutterstock, Gelpi; 6, Shutterstock, Jamzol;
7, Shutterstock, Kivrins Anatolijs; 8, Shutterstock, Matka Wariatka; 9, Shutterstock, Mandy
Godbehear; 10, Shutterstock, Stephen Finn; 11l, Shutterstock, Feng Yu; 11r, Shutterstock, Tischenko
Irina; 12, Shutterstock, HP Photo; 13, Shutterstock, Shootov Igor; 14, 29tl, Shutterstock, Ales Liska;
15t, Shutterstock, Simon Krzic; 15m, Shutterstock, Kamyshko; 15b, Shutterstock, Graham S. Klotz;
16c, Shutterstock, Gelpi; 16l, 29tr, Shutterstock, Florin Tirlea; 16c, Shutterstock, Lim Yong Hian;
17, Shutterstock, UKR Photo; 18, Shutterstock, David Hughes; 19, Shutterstock, Diligent;
20l, 28tl, Shutterstock, Iofoto; 20r, Shutterstock, Eric Gevaert; 21t, Shutterstock, Mike Flippo; 21b,
29b, Shutterstock, Jerry Horbert; 22, 28b, Shutterstock, Arne Trautmann; 24, Shutterstock,
Malibu Books; 25, Shutterstock, Gertjan Hooijer; 26, Shutterstock, Leah-Anne Thompson;
27, Shutterstock, Morgan Lane Photography.

Printed in China

Franklin Watts is a division of Hachette Children's Books, an Hachette UK company.
www.hachette.co.uk

Contents

Materials everywhere

Everything around you is made from a material.

▼

This kitchen is full of objects made from different sorts of materials.

glass　　　　　　　　**metal**

clay

paper

wood

Materials can be heavy or light, hard or soft, stiff or bendy, strong or weak.

soft plastic seat

strong metal frame

bendy rubber tyre

▲ Lots of materials have been used to make this bicycle.

Plastic

Plastic is a tough, light material. It is made in factories. Plastic can be made into many different shapes.

▲ **This plastic picnic set is hard and stiff.**

Some plastics are soft and squashy.

▲ **This air bed is made from squashy plastic.**

Metal

There are many types of metal.
Most metals are hard and shiny.
They are also very strong.

This crane is made of metal. It is used on a building site to lift heavy loads.

Metal can be made into different shapes or sharpened to make knives and tools.

aluminium can

steel knife, forks and spoons

▲ Aluminium and steel are two types of metal.

Clay

Clay is dug from the ground. Clay is soft and is used to make many things such as bowls and plates, and bricks for building houses.

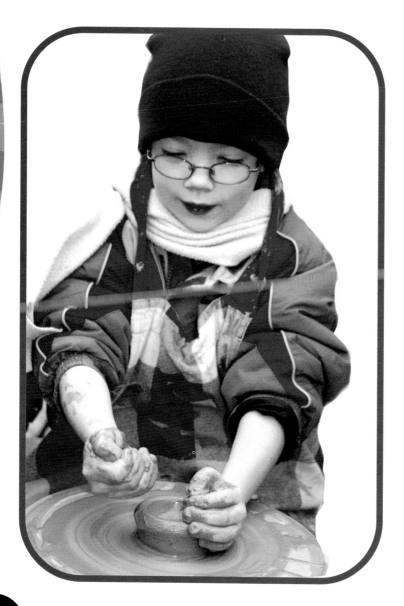

◀ **You can squash, press or roll clay into new shapes.**

Clay is baked in a very hot oven called a kiln. The clay dries out and becomes very hard.

▲ **These baked pots are strong and keep their shape. They can be used for lots of different things.**

Wood

Wood comes from trees. The trees are chopped down and the tree trunks are made into logs.

These logs will be sent to a factory where they will be made into different objects.

Wood can be cut, shaped and painted. Wood is used to make furniture and toys, and also to build houses.

▲ **The table, the tree and the Russian dolls are all made from wood.**

Paper

Paper is made from tiny pieces of wood mixed with water and chemicals to make a pulp. The pulp is then made into lots of different things.

Books, newspapers and brown bags are made from paper.

Paper can be used to make thick, strong cardboard. Boxes are made from cardboard.

▲ **What would happen if this box was made from thin paper?**

Glass

Glass is made by heating sand and some other materials together. You can see through glass. Glass is used to make things such as windows, bottles and jars.

Most glass is see-through and lets in light. Where is the glass in this picture?

Glass can be coloured. You can also paint on glass.

These glass bulbs are coloured but the light still shines through.

What you wear

Clothes can be made from wool and cotton. These are called natural materials.

◁ **A lot of our wool comes from sheep. A woollen jumper, scarf and gloves keep you warm in winter.**

sheep

Some of your clothes are made from plants. Cotton comes from the cotton plant.

▲ T-shirts made from cotton keep you cool when it is hot.

cotton plant

Plastic clothes

Lots of clothes are made from plastic materials. Nylon is a type of plastic material.

Some plastic materials are very tough, such as the plastic used in trainers. Some plastic materials are stretchy.

stretchy shorts

tough trainers

Some other plastic materials are waterproof. Plastic clothes can keep you dry when it is raining.

What would happen if this umbrella was made from wool?

The right materials

It is important to choose the right material for the right job.

clay roof tiles keep out the rain

wooden shutters can be closed to shut out the light

glass windows let in light

concrete walls give a strong shape

clay bricks make a path

▲ This house is built from many different materials.

This trampoline is made from metal and a very strong plastic material.

▼ **What would happen if this trampoline was made of paper?**

plastic

metal frame

Recycling

Using materials again to make new things is called recycling. When a material is recycled, it is turned into something new.

▼ **Lots of old, used objects can be recycled.**

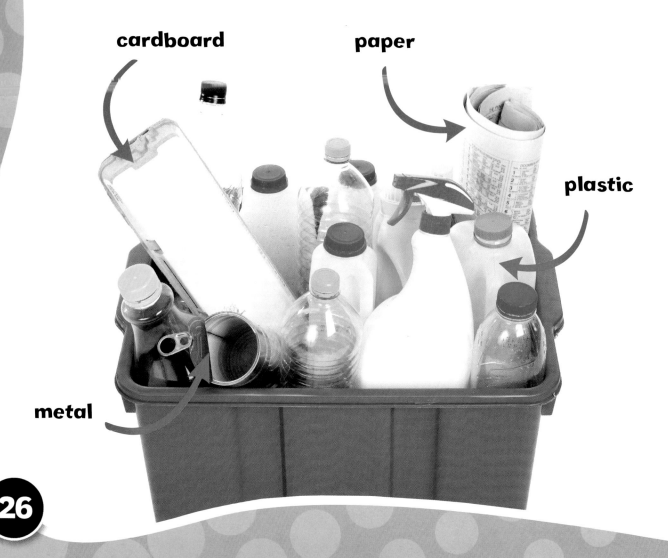

cardboard

paper

plastic

metal

Items can be recycled in all sorts of ways. Plastic bottles are recycled to make socks, plastic window frames and jewellery.

▼ **Try to recycle as much of your rubbish as possible.**

This sign means that used objects can be recycled or are made from recycled materials.

Things to do

Sheepish!

Which of these materials comes
from sheep?

a

b

c

Make a chair

Which of these things would you use to make a chair? Why?

a

b

c

Talk back

What material is this book made from?

What materials are you wearing?

How many metal things can you see?

How many glass things can you see?

Glossary

factory A building where things are made.

kiln A very hot oven used to bake objects made of clay to make them hard.

natural materials Any material that comes from plants, animals or the ground, such as clay, wood or wool.

pulp A wet, soggy mix made when wood is mixed with water.

Index